The Day the Whole World Stayed Home

Copyright © 2020 Kimberly Helleren
All rights reserved
First Edition

Fulton Books, Inc.
Meadville, PA

Published by Fulton Books 2020

ISBN 978-1-64952-428-7 (paperback)
ISBN 978-1-63710-473-6 (hardcover)
ISBN 978-1-64952-429-4 (digital)

Printed in the United States of America

The Day the Whole World Stayed Home

Written and Illustrated by
Kimberly Helleren

It started as a normal Tuesday. We were in circle with Mrs. Engelhart. She talked about taking home all our stuff. She told us about a special school bag for us to take home.
Did she say homework to do? What's that she said? It's not "take-home day." Our mommies and daddies were coming early to pick us up. Many parents showed up together.

We load up our backpacks, grab our nap bags, and say our goodbyes.
My mom and dad tell me we will be going right home. The parking lot is full, and all the kids have full backpacks.

When we got home from school, we look in the bag from my teacher.
We find a whiteboard, pens, color crayons, pencils, and lots of paper.
Wow, one of the pages has my name all over it.
Oh no, did my mom take home my morning skills practice sheet home?

The next morning, we have breakfast, but we are not getting ready for school. We watch our principal, Mrs. Jessie, and vice principal, Mrs. Angel, talking to us. They have their faith eyes on that they use for chapel. They pray over us and ask us to keep them in our prayers. We are to remember our faith eyes until we come back to school.

They say we are going to be doing our school work at home. They want us to work hard, and the teachers will be teaching us from the computer.

Later that day, Mrs. Lee shows up on the computer. She is showing us how to write our letters for the week. We need to get our whiteboard and pen. She wants us to follow along. She tells us to practice and be ready for tomorrow's lesson.

My brother and I match. We are in the same class. We are twins. We have each other to work and play with at home. We have the same lessons and teacher. When we are done playing, we find a book from school and read it together. We love to do things together.

Dad has made us a table to share. He is going to work from our home. We are going to share his computer. He calls me his coworker.
I take out my stuff and set up my workstation next to him.
We are ready to work.

Mommy says the mailman is working really hard and delivering everyone's mail.
I walk out to the mailbox and find a big envelope with my name on it.
I run inside and open it up.
It's from Mrs. Helleren, my art teacher.

It is paints, a crayon, a glue stick, and many pieces of paper. I look at the paper, and it shows our lessons from seven art elements around the seven continents. We were learning about the world before we left school. We had visited Asia and South America. Today is Africa. We are learning about lines and patterns from African fabric. I can't wait to start to make my project. There is a video on YouTube with Mrs. Helleren showing us what to do.
Hi, Mrs. Helleren!

My big brother and I finished all our lessons. Mom said, "Now it's time for PE." We are excited. We get to do a workout in our family room. We get to play loud music and move around.
We get hot and sweaty and need some water.

Mom wakes me up and spends time at breakfast with me. She lets me know she still has to go to work and help sick people. I will stay at home with my dad. She says she loves me and will see me tonight before I go to bed. We pray for our day and for all the sick people she will help today.

Mrs. Helleren had us share about our families.
She asked us to find out about our family traditions and bring back to share with our class. We have many friends around the world. My family is from Asia. My grandma lives with us. My mom and my grandma taught me to make very delicious food.
I can't wait to show and share what I did today to my class. I had so much fun, and it tasted very good.

I wave goodbye to my dad. I stay home to work on my schoolwork, but my dad has to work. He says he has to work for many families to get Wi-Fi at their homes so other kids can do school from home too.

My mom lets me help her work. She said I am doing a very important job helping keep our nurses and doctors safe. We have lots of colorful fabric. We are making very special face masks. I pick the fabric, and she sews them together. She delivers them to the hospital, and they are very thankful.

I wake up on a beautiful morning. My mom comes in, smiling. She said I need to get up and get ready. Today is the day that everyone goes back to school.

Won't my teacher be surprised how much I learned at home? I can't wait to see my teachers.

This is going to be a great day. This is the day we all go back to school!

This is the day the Lord has made.
We will rejoice and be glad in it.

—Psalm 118:24

About the Author

Kimberly Helleren has been a teacher for fourteen years and author of *The Day Everyone Stayed Home*. During the pandemic school shutdown, her students sent pictures and videos about their activities at home. She turned them into paintings and created a storybook from each family's experiences. She had her eleven-year-old niece help with painting the illustrations. Kimberly has used art for children to capture their creativity and enhance their learning. She has a big passion for every child to enjoy reading. Her husband, Leif, and sons, Svenn and Lars, have been great inspirations in her life. She plans to share many more children's adventures in the world around us.

CPSIA information can be obtained
at www.ICGtesting.com
Printed in the USA
LVRC061922290321
682857LV00001B/1